no god no son of god

no god no son of god

James Russell Sarver, Sr.

To order additional copies of this book, contact:
Xlibris Corporation
1-888-795-4274
www.Xlibris.com
Orders@Xlibris.com
117617

CONTENTS

Contradictions of the Bible

How could anyone believe that the earth is only 6000 years old, while science says it is billions of years old? Why did Moses not say anything about the other planets? That is because Moses did not know the other planets existed. How could there be trees, grasses, and herbs of the field on the earth on the third day, but there was no sun, moon, or stars until the fourth day? No living thing could exist for even one second without the sun. And the moon does not give off any light. It is just a reflection of the sun. Again, Moses did not know that How could any society exist coming from only 2 parents? How could an animal talk? I really kick myself for ever believing that a serpent could talk. How did Cain find the land of Nod, find a wife, and build a city with people in it? How could the arc be sealed from within and without? There would be no way for the waste to get out of the arc, no way for the gasses to escape.

THE TRUTH

According to the bible the earth is only 6,000 years old. Science says the earth is billions of years old. One person told me that there were two creations, one for prehistoric times and one for mankind.

Moses did not say anything about the other planets because Moses did not know they existed.

The fruit trees, grasses, and herbs of the field were upon the earth the third day, but no sun, moon, or stars until the fourth day. That is impossible. No living thing can exist without the sun. The moon does not give off any light, only a reflection of the sun. Dumb animals can not talk. There is no way that the serpent talked to Eve. The story of Cain was just plain silly. Where did all of those people come from? The arc was sealed with pitch from within and without. Nothing could get in. Nothing could get out. Where did all of the waste go? Where did all of the gasses go? The blacks of Austrailia have been there for 30,000 years. The tribes have been here for at least 20,000 years.

The bible is a farce, and there is no god.

Constantine forced christianity on the Romans, so he could control them Columbus landed in Central America. There were people there that he called, Indios, meaning god-like. One of these people fired an arrow into the shoulder of Americus Vesbusi (sp). That is how America got it's name. These people were not indians, natives, or American anything. They were the Tribes of Turtle Island. They were not destroyed by rifles. They were destroyed by white man's diseases. It is now known that Columbus caused the deaths of over 30 million of the men of Turtle Island. The whites are the most evil race of people on earth. They use christianity to control the tribes yet today. The government of the United States is extremely evil. They are using Aspartame to depopulate the world. One FDA official named Mike Delaney said, "What? We must depopulate!" Obama said that Delaney acted within the law. Aspartame is the most dangerous poison ever on earth. Aspartame causes almost every terrible and terminal disease and disorder known to man. Millions have died. Millions more will die unless Aspartame is stopped. Aspartame affects every system and every organ of the body. Does amybody want to know who was responsible for the deaths of the four Kennedys?

Hint: The Kennedys were supposed to destroy the money system.

P. S. The trees of Australia have been here 138,000 years

OTHER PLANTS

In the beginning God created the heaven and the earth. And the earth was without form, and void; and darkness was upon the face of the deep. And the spirit of God moved upon the face of the waters. Moses says nothing about Mercury, Venus, Mars, Jupiter, Saturn, Neptune, Uranus, or Pluto. All of these are part of creation. However, Moses could not see them, so they are not in his form of creation. Moses speaks about two great lights. There is only one great light. The moon does not give off any light. This is just a reflection of the sun. Moses only wrote about the sun, moon stars, and earth, only what he knew existed. Moses also believed that the sun revolved around the earth. Somehow, the biblical creation has a form of light even before the sun. How can this be? According to doctrine this light was Jesus Christ. What kind of garbage is this? Do you have any idea how much light it would take to light up the entire world? Twice in my life I suffered the same attack. I was sitting on a straight—back chair in my dingy old apartment on Jefferson Street in Crawfordsville, In. I read about the fruit trees, grasses, and herbs of the field being upon the earth the third day, while there was no sun, moon, or stars until the fourth day. I flipped over backwards, landing on my face, almost threw up, cried like a baby beat my fists into the floor, and trembled for two days. I had the exact same reaction when I read about Mark saying that Peter would deny knowing Jesus thrice before the cock crows twice. The cock did not crow twice. The cock only crowed once. It did not crow after the first denial of Peter as Mark says, only after the third denial. Mark was a punk kid. His real name was John Mark. Mark was called Mark so he would not be confused with the disciple John. Mark was the kid who escaped naked in the wilderness. Again, Mark was a punk kid. Mark had no business writing the gospel. Mark screwed everything up.

All you have to do is read the bible with an open mind You will see that there is no god, and Jesus did not die. Why was I able to figure all of this out? It is because I am bipolar. I can see way past what others can see. Why would I make such a great President? Like Ike I have never been in a public office and I do not owe any labor union, GM, Ford, Chrysler, Standard Oil, Railroad, Big Banks, etc a dime. Like Richard Milhouse Nixon I have great diplomacy with foreign nations. Finally, like Ronald Wilson Reagan I will not take any shit off of anyone. With just a few moves I could straighten out this country so it would be as great as it was during the time of President Dwight David Eisenhour. Democrats say that the times made Ike. I say Ike made the times.

The Races Verses Evolution

A well-educated second grader should be able to figure this out. However, they can not because their minds are poisoned by the words of the bible. Evolution is one particular species changing out of necessity or because of their environment. Actually, it was the bible that enabled me to see the truth. The three sons of Noah were suppose to represent the three different races. Ham's people were black and lived in Africa. Shem's people were yellow and lived in Asia. Japheth's people were white and lived in Europe. Again, there would have been one man and one woman starting each society. If one man and one woman were responsible for the entire society we would not be able to talk, write, or even play basketball. The original people on earth were not any particular race. Many of these people migrated to Africa, many to Asia and many to Europe. Because of the hot rays of the sun in Africa the Africans needed more mellanon (sp) in their blood. Our slaves were as black as the ace of spades. I always wondered why they called themselves blacks The are now brown. Maybe you can remember the story about the two small brother and sister. that got lost in Africa. I saw pictures of them. I just about dropped my teethThese two children looked like Africans. Evidently, evolution reacts quickly in the hot African sun. The people of Asia and Europe did not need as much protection from the sun, weather conditions, and other elements of earth. Flowers did not have nectar. They needed something to attract the attract the insects and hummingbirds for pollination. This is a very simple form of evolution. In case you have not noticed girls have much bigger breasts today. Girls are also starting their menstrual cycle as early as seven or eight. What is the reason for this? Egg layers only allow their hens one hour of darkness each night. Hens are popping eggs out like they are going out of style. Our homes , businesses, factories, etc. all have lights. Lights are what is causing the big breasts and our little girls to start their menstrual cycles so soon. I call this artificial evolution. I am going to go way out on a limb. I say that our Negro people here in the U. S. will be nearly as white as I am in two hundred years or so. Furthermore, human beings did not evolve from monkeys, apes, or any other animal, and we did not come from the amibe (sp)

JOSHUA

Joshua was the given name of Jesus. Joshua was not called Jesus, Christ, or Jesus Christ until he was 30 years old. Joshua was not born in December. He was not born between October and February, as there were flowers in bloom. Joshua was born in the spring. The Day Jesus Did Not Die! It was daylight when the Jews held their council. There were many false witnesses. That took time. The Jews wanted to get Jesus on the cross as soon as possible. Remember, there was no form of transportation. They walked Jesus to see Pilate. Pilate had been warned by his wife to have nothing to do with Jesus. Pilate heard one of the Jews say that Jesus was preaching all over Gallalee. . So Pilate sent Jesus to King Herod. . Herod spoke to Jesus with many words. Herod wanted Jesus to perform a miracle, but Jesus just stood there. Finally, Herod turned Jesus over to his soldiers. The put a robe on Jesus. They bounced him around for a while. (Anybody watching the time?)Here we go again. We go back to Pilate. Watch all that happens here. Pilate says At that feast you have a custom. What feast? The first feast ended at sun up. Here comes the story of Barrabas. They have to go way back in the prison to get him. Now, watch this. Jesus is scourged. You talk about time. A man is whipped within in an inch of his life. Then they pluck his beard out one whisker at a time. It was the preparation of the passover and about the sixth hour. (John 19:14) Jesus is still in front of Pilate, and they have not even started the slow walk to Calvary. The sixth hour is NOON. I Thirst They put some hyssop up to the lips of Jesus. The hyssop contained some kind of poison. Jesus went into a deep sleep. In the coolness of the sepulchre Jesus woke up. Jesus never died. Jesus and Mary Magdalene net in the garden. Eventually, tey went off together. Rumor has it that they went to France. I have no idea, but I have always known that they were very much in love with each other.

Who Were They

They were the first people on earth. No, they were not Adam and Eve. If the human race had come from only one man and one woman we would not be able to read, write, or even play basketball. There would be no cars, planes, or trains. There is only one way that it could have happened. There were many of them. There was no such thing as race. Who created them? Nobody created them. Like all plants and animals they were the product of chemical processes, especially carbon . . . Do I know who they were? YES, I DO!!! They were all . . . .

Aspartame Poisoning Plus

Aspartame is the most dangerous poison ever on earth!!!If you continue to consume products containing Aspartame you will die from Aspartame Poisoning. Aspartame is 50% phenylalanine (an amino acid), 40% aspartic acid (another amino acid), and 10% METHYL ALCOHOL (the most dangerous alcohol known to man). Aspartame affects every organ and every system of the body. * * * Little Chastity was born a beautiful baby girl. However, her parents had consumed products containing Aspartame. Because of this Chastity received male hormones. The reproductive system is a fine and intricate system. It can not handle any dangerous chemicals such as Aspartame. Aspartame causes many different birth defects, including autism, cleft palate, and even SIDS. * * * Millions have died all over the world from Aspartame Poisoning. The government is using Aspartame to depopulate the world. Michael Deleny of the FDA was quoted as saying, "What?" "We need to depopulate!" Obama said that Delaney acted within the law. *   *   * Aspartame causes ALS, Alzheimers, arthritis, asthma, birth defects, all cancers, sudden

death, dizziness, epilepsy, fibromyalgia, severe headaches, heart disease, inner ear and balance problems, liver disorders, leukemia, lupus kidney disorders. mental disorders (especially bipolar disorder and straight depression), M. S. , obesity (Aspartame affects the pancreas, causing the body to crave carbohydrates, causing obesity and sugar diabetes), Parkinsons, strokes, sugar diabetes, and thyroid disorder. This is a partial list. I am sure there are others. * * * Please, Please, Please do not chew sugar free gum. ? ! The dreaded poison will go through the saliva, straight to the brain, and cause brain cancer.

THE DEATHS OF
THE FOUR KENNEDYS

Joseph Patrick Kennedy was to be Vice President. He was a great pilot, and he volunteered for a special mission. He was to fly a bomber loaded with explosives into the channel. At a certain point Joe was to push a button, ejecting him from the bomber. The bomber was to fly on by itself and explode. Once the Kennedys got into power they were to change the monetary system of the United States. The British bankers could not have this happen. The British bankers had Joe's bomber rigged. So, when Joe Pushed the button the bomber blew up. Joseph Patrick Kennedy, Sr. wanted to investigate the situation, but the government said that Joe, Sr. did not have high enough clearance. That is how Joe, Jr died John F Kennedy won the democrat nomination in Chicago in 1960. However, it was not fair. Bobby Kennedy, who was running the show, told John that he had to leave for a while and John was to choose any Vice President but Lyndon Baines Johnson. After Bobby left LBJ took JFK into an empty office. There he told JFK how they could pool their illegal voters and defeat Richard Milhouse Nixon. They came out of the empty office and JFK announced that LBJ would be his running mate. Bobby came back and threw a tremendous fit. LBJ hated Bobby after that. Six days before the election election officials made Kennedy and Nixon sign an agreement that neither would contest the results of the election. That turned loose all of the Kennedy and Jonson illegal voters to vote as many times as they wanted. Over 100 million voted in 1060. Find them for me. You would be lucky to find 80 million live, legal, and registered voters. Richard Milhouse Nixon actually won the 1960 election by a landslide. I spoke to an old election official named Vaught. I told him that there were not anywhere near 100 million voters in 1960. Vaught agreed. I asked him why nothing was done. He said, "We were afraid we would cause a panic." My reply was, "What do you call the so-called peaceful demonstrations of the 60s "*   *   * Here we go again. The British bankers got a hold of LBJ to have JFK assassinated. LBJ contacted Cord Mayer(sp), and everything fell into place. One man was resonible for making sure that the limosine turned. It was suppose to go straight. There were three men arrested on the Grassy Knoll. The mayor of Dallas told his police to let these men loose. That is because the mayor of Dallas was in on the assassination. The brother of the mayor was a general, and JFK fired him. Lee Harvey Oswald did not kill JFK. The man who killed JFK was Lucien Sarti. He said, I killed your President. Get over it."

I saw the doctor on television who first saw JFK after he was shot. He pointed to the small of his throat and said that the bullet that killed Kennedy hit him right here and exited out the back of his head. I saw the autopsy photos. That was not a pleasant sight. Lucien Sarti shot Kennedy at the almost opposite angle that Oswald shot . . .*   *   * Mary Mayor, the wife of Cord Mayor, got JFK stoned on cocaine and screwed his legs off. By the way, there were many drug parties in the white house while Kennedy was President. That should tell you how evil the Kennedys were. Bobby knew about the affair with Mary. Mary was out jogging when a man wearing a windbreaker and a golf cap shot her in the back of the head

One very horrible thing that happened was that the democrats rode the coat tails of Kennedy and Johnson into Congress. These worthless democrats are the reason our country is in such bad shape today. The voters did not get into power any decent senators or congressmen. *   *   * Many times when I read a book I only get one or two statements out of the whole book. This was true of a book, Four Days, a book I found in my parent's basement. All I got out of this book was one statement. That statement was that JFK confided in LBJ anything that he was going to do. So, LBJ knew that JFK planned to withdraw all troops from Viet Nam. LBJ could not have that Ladybird owned all kinds of stock in the company that was sending all of the helicopters and tanks over there. Ladybird would have lost millions if Kennedy withdrew all troops from Viet Nam. Once in power LBJ looked for ways to escalate the war. There were two destroyers in the Gulf. One was the Maddox. The other was the Sea Turner Joy. One fired on the other, and the other fired back. They both radioed back to the United States that they had been fired upon on the high seas. The Viet Cong had no weapons that could hurt a destroyer. The worthless Congress voted to escalate the war, and thousands of Marines hit the beaches of Viet Nam the next morning. IMPOSSIBLE! Only if the troops had already been deployed could have this happened. Toward the end of WW2 they were thinking about sending Patton to Japan and use agent orange. Ike said no.

Field Marshall Montgomery said no. Even Joseph Stalin said no to using agent orange. The only man ever ruthless enough to use agent orange was Lyndon Baines Johnson. To make matters worse our soldiers were not allowed to have bullets for their weapons. I knew an M. P. who did not even have bullets for his weapons. Thousands of our men were killed sitting around the camp fire. *   *   * Here we go again. Bobby went one way, and his bodyguards went the other. This was planned. Bobby was face to face with Sirhan Sirhan. Sirhan shot at Bobby with a . 25 caliper pea shooter. Only a direct hit to the head or one to the heart could have been lethal. They have always known that there were two different caliper bullets fired at Bobby. I do not know for sure who killed Bobby. I have a S. W. A. G. That is a scientific wild ass guess. I believe that it was Cord Mayor. Whoever killed Bobby got way down low and fired upwards, hitting Bobby behind his ear and piercing his brain.

*   *   * JFK, Jr was not a great pilot. However, he was not an absolute idiot either. Like Joe , Jr the plane was worked over by someone. It did not just go down. Again, I do not know who was responsible, but it was no accident. It was caused. The Kennedys had the knack of forming enemies in low places.

Jim Sarver For President 2012

The seat belt law shall be repealed or be held unconstitutional. Nobody should be forced to wear a seat belt. Americans have the right to life, liberty, and the pursuit of happiness. All of these are destroyed by the seat belt law. Our streets, highways, and byways are not the Indy 500 or the Daytona 500. All drivers that I have seen that believe in seat belts are tailgaters. Tailgating is what causes most deaths and accidents. Drivers should be required to keep a distance of one car length for every ten miles per hour from the car in front of them. Besides all of this, the seat belt law is unconstitutional. *   *   * All labor unions and any general facsimiles, including sports, shall be made illegal. Non labor union workers better, faster, and cheaper. We could save billions on our highways alone *   *   * The chapter seven bankruptcy would be for medical reasons only. Nobody can control sickness or injury. *   *   * The jury system is to be changed from twelve out of twelve to nine out of twelve *   *   * The penalty for rape, child molesting, murder, kidnapping, robbery, burglary, and PERJURY shall be death. Criminals have no rights. Police may use any methods to achieve an arrest except lies *   *   * There will be no smoking in any enclosed area except bars or taverns *   *   * Aspartame is banned. Anyone caught using, buying, or selling any product containing Aspartame shall be fined 10,000 dollars and spend ninety days in jail. *   *   * All Americans may own pistols, rifles, shotguns, bows and arrows, and crossbows. No American can own any automatic weapon, machine guns, flame throwers, bazookas, cannons, tanks, or any other weapon designated for the police or military. Any such weapons may be turned into the local sheriff or police department. *   *   * No money, for any reason, at any time, may be taken from social security. *   *   * All homes, businesses, and farms shall use Shaklee products. No chemical fertilizers, herbicides, or pesticides shall be used. Shaklee's Basic

H is a great fertilizer and pesticide. Shaklee products will purify our rivers and streams. *   *   * Anyone caught throwing cigarette butts, cigarette packs, glass products, plastic products, metal products, or garbage on the soil, sidewalks, streets, byways, or highways shall pay a 10,000 dollar fine and spend ninety days in jail. *   *   * Men have run our government for centuries. Our government is in bad shape. . It is high time to give our women a chance to run the show. From the Vice President down all positions of authority are to be women. That includes the President's cabinet, CIA, FBI, FDA, FAA, Secret Service, Senate, House of Representatives, etc. *   *   * Freedom of speech and freedom of the press Depends on the truth *   *   * There is to be no tax on tobacco, alcohol, or gasoline. I promise the price of gasoline will go way down. I know exactly how to do it. My tax will be the sales tax, the only fair tax. *   *   * English is the official language of the United States of America. . Only English will be spoken, read, and written in America (except the tribes). Anyone caught using another language shall be deported. The border patrol between the border of the United States and Mexico shall be increased by three times, and all immigration into the United States shall cease Patrol officers shall have permission to use their weapons *   *   * For safety sake all nuclear plants will be shut down. The space program will also be shut down. We did not lose anything in outer space. *   *   * Finally, because our children watch television, there is to be no more R rated shows and movies on television.

The Economy Part 1

The cause of the trillion dollar debt is twofold. The first cause is a simple one but very costly to the bankers and taxpayers. It is the chapter seven bankruptcy. The only bankruptcy that should be allowed is for medical reasons. Nobody can control getting sick or injured, and high medical bills can devastate an individual or an entire family. However, charging $10,000 to a credit card and forcing te taxpayer to cover it is an atrocity. Burt Reynolds has filed bankruptcy at least twice that I know. Donald Trump files bankruptcy more often than I change my underwear. . Wake up, America! It is time to smell the coffee. It is time to stop the chapter seven bankruptcy. *   *   *

The second cause of our tremendous national debt is more complicated. It has been a national embarrassment for centuries . . . The democrats have protected this worthless atrocity for as many years, and they have made a fortune off of it. Our national debt will continue to rise as long as this organization is allowed to exist. There is absolutely no way possible that we can ever, ever get back in the black. *   *   * This is the labor union and general facsimilies, including sports. Ball players, golfers, tennis players, soccer players, race car drivers, etc are paid millions of dollars each to play a game. What is wrong with this picture? Men actually get paid to make sure that this happens. Ball players should not make more than $100,000 per year. Then, all of the moms and dads could take their kids to see a ball game. They could still feed their family for the next month, and we could eliminate the men who make a fortune selling the the ball players to the owners for a rediculous price. This is the same thing as a labor union only with a different name. *   *   * It is a federal law that all federal government contracts must be fulfilled by labor union labor. This is costing the taxpayers billions of dollars every year. Non labor union workers are faster, better, and cheaper. We could save billions of dollars every year on highway construction alone and have better roads to boot. That is saying nothing about all of the Federal buildings that are built every year, plus other government spending. *   *   *

The United States Postal Service is a joke. Look how often the price of a simple postage stamp has gone up. This is because of the labor union . . . *   *   * The railroad is another labor union embarrassment. Have you ever watched railroad labor union workers work? i worked for Cargill, Inc of Linden, IN. My job was to load train cars and trucks. Many times I would stand in my load out shanty for as much as 24 hours at a time. I was able to look out and watch those lazy railroad workers work. , and I use the term loosely. There was one very old man wearing a white undershirt working his tail off. The rest of the crew, including the foreman, were standing around smoking cigarettes and telling jokes.

THE ECONOMY PART 2

We had to work closely with the railroad because there was a special union crew that was on call to bring the rail cars into our yard so I could load them. I was talking to one worker who said that if he did not come when he was called he did not get paid. He said that was wrong and that he should get paid whether he showed up for work or not. I was dumbfounded. That was a normal outlook for a union man. *   *   * Twice the crew refused to bring us our cars. One time the locomotive did not have a light bulb. We had to wait for hours for an electrician to replace that light bulb. The other time when the crew got there they decided to take a break. When they finally decided to go back to work the engineer switched locomotives. The one he chose did not have a seat. So, again, we had to wait. I overheard the crew talking. They figured that the maintenance man would come and take one of the seats out of another locomotive and put it into the locomotive the engineer was in. Dig this plan. The engineer was then going to get into the locomotive that would now have no seat. Their plan failed because the maintenance man brought a seat with him. That crew was madder than an old wet hen. They were forced to bring the cars to us. *   *   * This crew decided to go on strike. Cargill had loaded cars that needed to go out. . I threw the switch to the main line. Five of us piled into Cargill's locomotive and moved those loaded cars out onto the main line so the regular train could pick them up. That was illegal. We were not allowed to throw that switch, but our boss asked us to do it because those loaded cars were needed. Four of us lid on the floor of the locomotive. Our engineer got as flat as he could on his seat. Those strikers had guns. Labor unions can kill, rape, steal, or anything else in the name of a labor union, and nobody will touch them. *   *   * General Motors, Chrysler, and Ford can all tell you stories about how production can be stopped. I am going to allow them to tell you some of their stories. I am sure that they can keep you laughing for a long time. *   *   * The man who designed the economy of Japan. was an

American. He knew one thing for certain There would not be any labor unions in Japan. This is the single reason why Japan keeps getting ahead of us. If we get rid of labor unions we will go of Japan. It will make their heads spin. . As long as we have labor unions we will continue, and continue, and continue to go deeper and deeper into the red. Labor unions have been our downfall for centuries . . . the democrats have made sure of that. * * * The labor union bosses sit on their asses, ratchet-jawed on their phones, and have never helped in any to produce an American product. They are just a suck off our economy. * * * Jimmy Carter would not stop the coal strike. Many of our elderly died sitting next to their stoves. I think about this often because I have such a tremendous amount of respect for our older Americans. I am very much in support of a law that would make it impossible for the democrats to touch, for any reason, or any time any money in the Social Security Fund. It is 100% impossible to have a surplus in the Social Security Fund.

Joseph Patrick Kennedy, Sr.

Al Capone was the most known criminal in U. S. history. Yet, Joe Kennedy, Sr. did everything he did without being in jail for one minute. Bobby Kennedy performed a huge criminal investigation and run into his own father. Joe was the ambassador to England. He told Hitler when, where, and how to bomb England. He did get caught. He said that England was a protestant nation and that he hated Protestants. He should have been executed for high treason. However, it was Kennedy money that got FDR elected. Nothing was done to him. He taught his children well. They would bum for their milk money, lunch money, pop money, etc. They showed no remorse if this caused the other children a problem. They were just that evil even as children. This, along with the story of the Cuban Missile Crisis(JFK made a compromise with Russia two weeks before his famous statement) and the fact that he was going to withdraw all troops from Viet Namwas on the national news. Without a doubt, the 1964 Civil Rights Act is the worst thing that ever happened to the American people.

PEARL HARBOR
NO SURPRISE

Pearl Harbor was about as much of a surprise as the sun coming up. FDR knew for days that Japan was going to bomb Pearl Harbor, but he did not warn are Navy. FDR knew that if Japan attacked Pearl Harbor Congress would declare war. All of those men and ships sunk to make money, not for freedom. I talked to many of the witnesses and read other accounts. They all had the same story. They saw the planes coming many miles away, but could not get the attention of our Navy. The reason was simple. All the Navy were drunk. I will bet you that I can tell you who supplied the alcohol. FDR wanted to make sure that our Navy could not defend itself. All of those men and ships went to the bottom of the ocean in order to line the pockets of certain people. If you get the chance read the accounts about Pearl Harbor. You will find that the attack was no surprise, just no officers to order our sailors to fire the big guns. My Dad said that he would have fired the guns any way. Unfortunately, it does not work that way.

SNAKE BITE

Had it been a snake it would have bit me. I could not figure out why the democrats keep winning. The answer is simple-illegal voters. In a biography of Bobby Kennedy it states that two men came up to Joe, Sr and stated that they had each voted 122 today. That was not the 60 election. So, I spaced it for a while. All of the experts said that Ted Kennedy would lose his last election. I could not believe it when Ted won. The Kennedys backed Obama. So, you can bet that Obama received Kennedy illegal votes. All of this goes back a long time. That is how the democrats keep winning. The main illegal votes come from the Kennedys and the Johnsons. There have been 100s, possibly 1000s of democrats that have used. No wonder the democrats keep winning.

THE 1964 CIVIL RIGHTS ACT

The 1964 Civil Rights Act is the worst thing that ever happened to the American people. Employers were unable to hire decent help. They could only hire inexperienced blacks and women. Production quantity went to hell. Production quality was even worse. Men could not find work to support their families. Mass divorce followed. Women became sluts and whores/Children wondered what man was going to be in their home tonight. The Cat's In The Cradle and Skip A Rope were songs of my generation screaming out in pain and agony. I sat and listened to the children. The family went to hell. Children never knew whether they were going to be with a grandmother or a babysitter. I have attempted to keep this story as easy and simple as I can. There really is not an easy way to explain just how terrible the 1964 Civil Rights Act was. Next you had integration. You just as well put the kids in schools, block the doors and windows, and turn some starving tigers loose on them. You could not have done any more harm. The 1964 Civil Rights Act is without a doubt the worst thing to ever happen to the American people. Free Sex, just what Kennedy wanted.

MY HERO,
ABRAHAM LINCOLN

My first hero was Buffalo Bill Cody. Then, I found out that Cody did nothing but nearly make the Buffalo extinct. My new hero became Abraham Lincoln. I studied Lincoln for many years. I did book report after book report about Abe. I just could not get enough information about him. I was completely against slavery, and I thought Lincoln was the greatest for freeing the slaves Then, I found out the truth. I studied Lincoln. Through his bipolar condition, nobody in history has been more bipolar than Abraham Lincoln. The history books will tell you that Lincoln's wife caused him to go crazy. Actually the opposite is true. It was Lincoln who caused his wife to go crazy. Lincoln believed that the government was like a god. Had Lincoln not been assassinated there would have been another Civil War because Lincoln believed that you needed his permission to go to the bath room. The reason for the Civil War was the northern businessmen wanted to go down to the south, take away the agricultural land, and build factories on the land, making slaves out of the rebels, just like the men in the north were already. Slavery had absolutely nothing to do with the war. The north had a 3 to 1 advantage over the south. The north had repeating rifles. They had plenty of food and dry clothing. Lincoln called a meeting with his advisors and generals because he could not understand why the Union Army could not defeat the rebels. The advisors and generals told Lincoln that the reason that the North could not defeat the South was that the slaves were fighting along with the South, and if he did mot free the slaves they were going to lose the war. Most Americans already hated Lincoln because without the right to leave the Union there would never been a Union. According to the history books the South fired the first shot. Wrong! Jefferson Danis was in the Supreme Court going through the legal process of leaning the Union. Lincoln had to get the war started NOW!~Lincoln could not say that he was going to free the slaves in order to defeat the South, so he made up the biggest lie ever told in America, The Emancipation Proclamation, Lincoln signed all legislation, A Lincoln. He hated the name, Abraham. It was a biblical name, and he did not believe in god. He only read the bible because it was something to read. He signed the Emancipation Proclamation, Abraham Lincoln, proving that it was a lie. If you want more ask me in person.

I sure hope you received the article about Lincoln. Anytime I write what I consider an extremely important e-mail the computer screws up. I consider the article about Lincoln Continued the most important thing I have ever written. I have known about slavery since I was in High School. Like many things people just space things for some reason, like Columbus naming America after Americus Vespucci (sp). Slavery was the losers of tribal wars in Africa. The white man had absolutely nothing to do with slavery. Their own people sold them into slavery. For centuries the black man has blamed the white man for becoming slaves. That just is not so. It is a real shame that the blacks have decided the white man and others are responsible for their fate. It is high time that the blacks accept the fact that their own people sold them into slavery. Furthermore, they need to know that Lincoln did not free them on a moral note, but only did so in order to defeat the Confederacy. Another thing that we need to do is disband the KKK. The KKK has no purpose, and can only harm both the whites and the blacks. This has been rough on me. I am in tears as I write this. Lincoln was my hero. By the way, Lincoln's assassination was a conspiracy. They tried to blame Jefferson Davis, General Robert Edward Lee, many Confederate officers, and others. It is easy to figure out who killed Lincoln. Just look at the ones who suffered the most. Lincoln let the South back in without penalty. The northern businessmen had shoveled all kinds of money into the Union Army and got absolutely nothing in return. It was the northern businessmen who had Lincoln killed. They found a man with red hair that had John Wilkes Booth papers on him. They executed him. As far as I know, and I could be wrong, they never found Booth. At this point I would like to bring up two things. Lincoln would have never made it through his term. He suffered from being a giant. Also JFK, as I understand, suffered from Parkinson's. Neither would have made it through their term.

Sarver's Plan For America

For the last sixty years our President and Congress has been decided by illegal votes. This is especially true for the Kennedys and Lyndon Johnson. This is not fair to the American people and the Republican Party since this has all been done by the democrat party. In order to make everything fair it is my idea to repeal all laws passed after John Kennedy took office. Good republicans would be put into the House of Representatives, and good republicans would be put into the senate. Then decent legislation; would be passed. It is obvious that the democrat party should be placed on some form of probation until they can be trusted by the American people.

UNREAL

When I first started writing this book I knew that there were many illegal votes cast in 1960. Now I have found that the democrats used their illegal voting system before FDR. This is UNREAL. I have heard some people say that they thought that their vote counted. I do not see how this is possible, especially the republicans. The democrat illegal voting machine goes back 75 years, and has been used as late as the Obama election and the Ted Kennedy election. This certainly is unreal to me. I wonder how much longer the democrats intend to use it.

NOTES

NOTES

NOTES

NOTES

NOTES

NOTES

NOTES

NOTES

NOTES

NOTES

NOTES

NOTES

NOTES

NOTES

NOTES

NOTES

NOTES

NOTES

NOTES

NOTES

JAMES SARVER

FOR

PRESIDENT

The election of 1948 was a tragedy. The headlines of the newspaper read that Dewey defeated Truman. The headlines were correct. However, Kennedy illegal votes gave the election to Truman. That was a real shame, as in 1951, Truman fired General Douglas MacArthur. In April of 1964 General MacArthur passed away. I had never seen my mother cry. On that day I saw my mother cry all day long. The United States Army only recognizes two Generals as their entire base. Those two Generals are Lee and MacArthur. This time Kennedy's illegal votes really caused a problem. The movie industry has tried to produce a movie about Truman, but the just can none get the job done. There are way too many people that hate Truman.